The Bedtime Song

t
tate publishing
CHILDREN'S DIVISION

WANDA SPEARS

Published by Tate Publishing & Enterprises, LLC
127 E. Trade Center Terrace | Mustang, Oklahoma 73064 USA
1.888.361.9473 | www.tatepublishing.com

Tate Publishing is committed to excellence in the publishing industry. The company reflects the philosophy established by the founders, based on Psalm 68:11,
"The Lord gave the word and great was the company of those who published it."

Book design copyright © 2016 by Tate Publishing, LLC. All rights reserved.
Cover and interior design by Rhezette Fiel
Illustrations by Michael Bermundo

Published in the United States of America

ISBN: 978-1-68028-908-4
Juvenile Nonfiction / General
15.10.27

This book is dedicated to my grandmother Ruth Eva Hayes Smith, my mother, Darryal Beverly Smith Hook, my Aunts Mabel, Jacqueline, Barbara, and my godmother Geraldine. "The Bedtime Song" was sung to me by all of them when I was a little girl, and this song continues to be passed on to the children in our family.

Two eyes

that shine

so bright

Two lips
that kiss
good night

Two arms
that hold
me tight

That sweet baby of mine

Two cheeks

just like

a rose

One turned up

shiny nose

You're sweet from

head to toe

That sweet baby of mine

Nobody

will ever

know

Just what your

coming has meant

Oh gee

I love you

so

You're something

Heaven has sent

You'll climb upon

my knee

You're all the

world to me

To me

you'll always be

That sweet

BABY

of mine

_____

Name

_____

Age

_____

Date

_____

Read to me by

About the Author

Wanda Spears was born in New Orleans, Louisiana, and grew up in the military. Her father was in the United States Air Force, and she was blessed to have lived in many places all over the world with her mother, sister, and brother.

She graduated from John F. Kennedy High School and earned two associate degrees. She worked at Tulane University and for a healthcare company—each for nearly fifteen years—before she began writing children's books.

Her inspiration for writing came from her grandson Pierce. She currently resides in Plano, Texas, with her husband, Alex. She has three children—Krystina, Alexandra, and Jacob.

Collect Other
Timeless Memories Titles

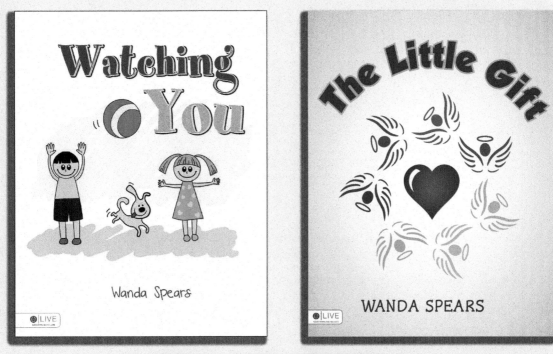

listen|imagine|view|experience

AUDIO BOOK DOWNLOAD INCLUDED WITH THIS BOOK!

In your hands you hold a complete digital entertainment package. In addition to the paper version, you receive a free download of the audio version of this book. Simply use the code listed below when visiting our website. Once downloaded to your computer, you can listen to the book through your computer's speakers, burn it to an audio CD or save the file to your portable music device (such as Apple's popular iPod) and listen on the go!

How to get your free audio book digital download:

1. Visit www.tatepublishing.com and click on the e|LIVE logo on the home page.
2. Enter the following coupon code:
   892f-34aa-7ab6-56ad-b0cc-58db-cbd0-8d7c
3. Download the audio book from your e|LIVE digital locker and begin enjoying your new digital entertainment package today!

CPSIA information can be obtained
at www.ICGtesting.com
Printed in the USA
LVOW01s1350080716

495511LV00006B/15/P